This book belongs to:

____

Draw as you wish:

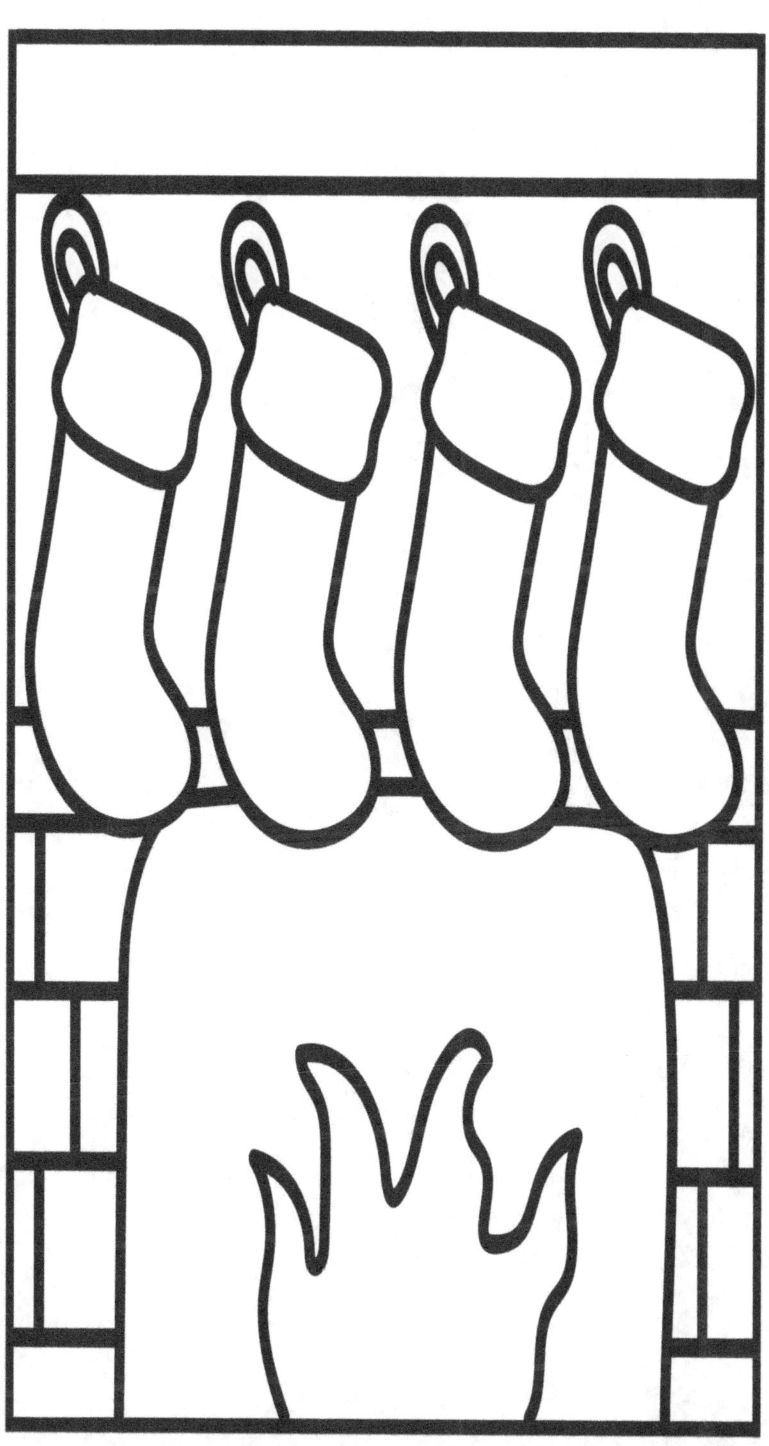

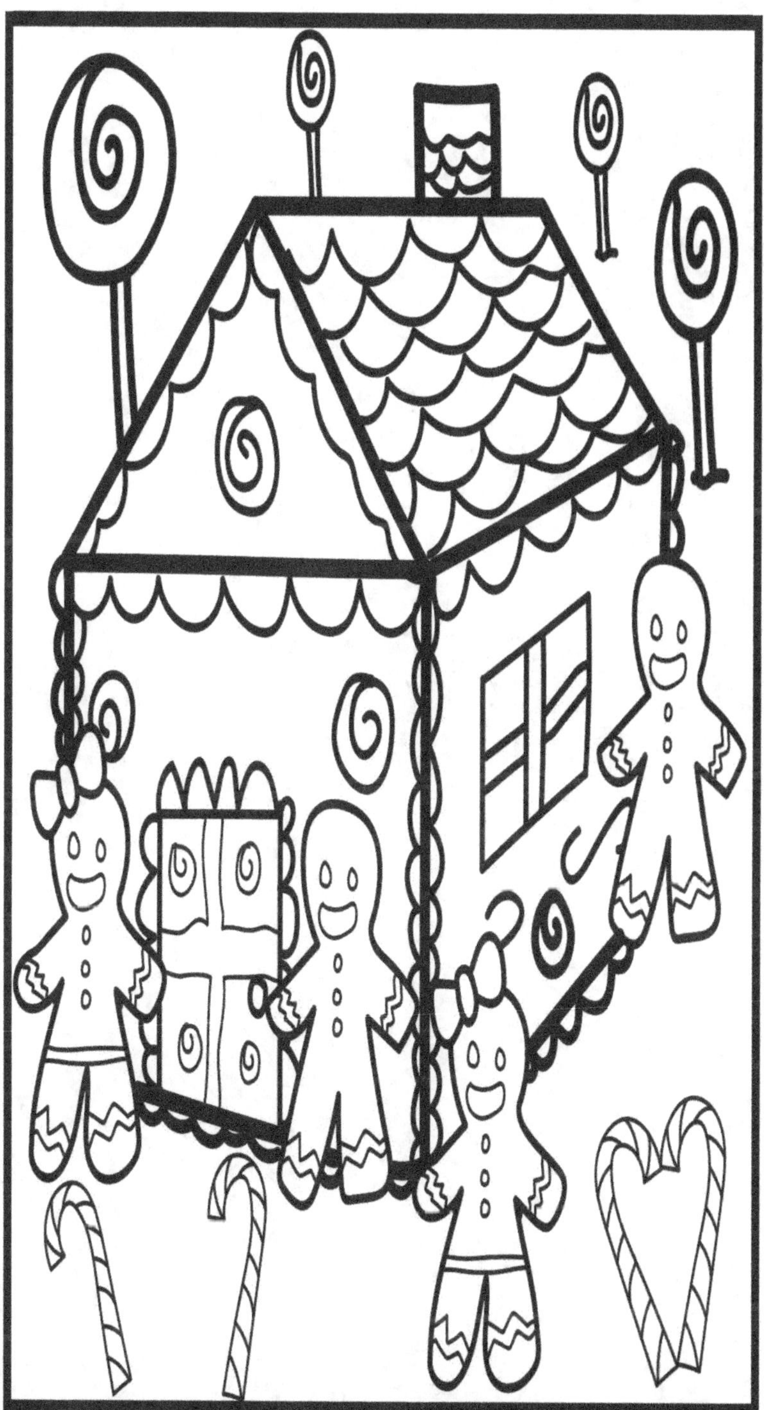

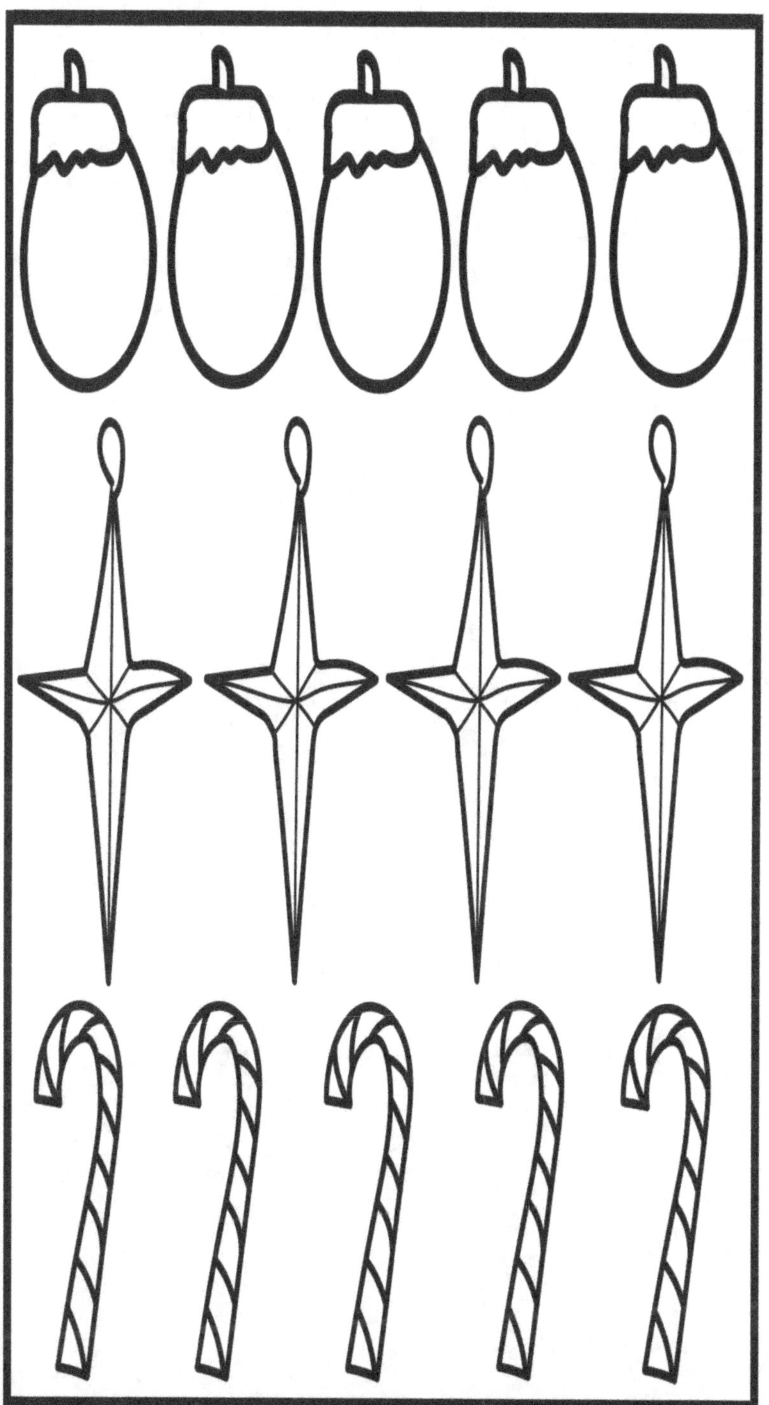

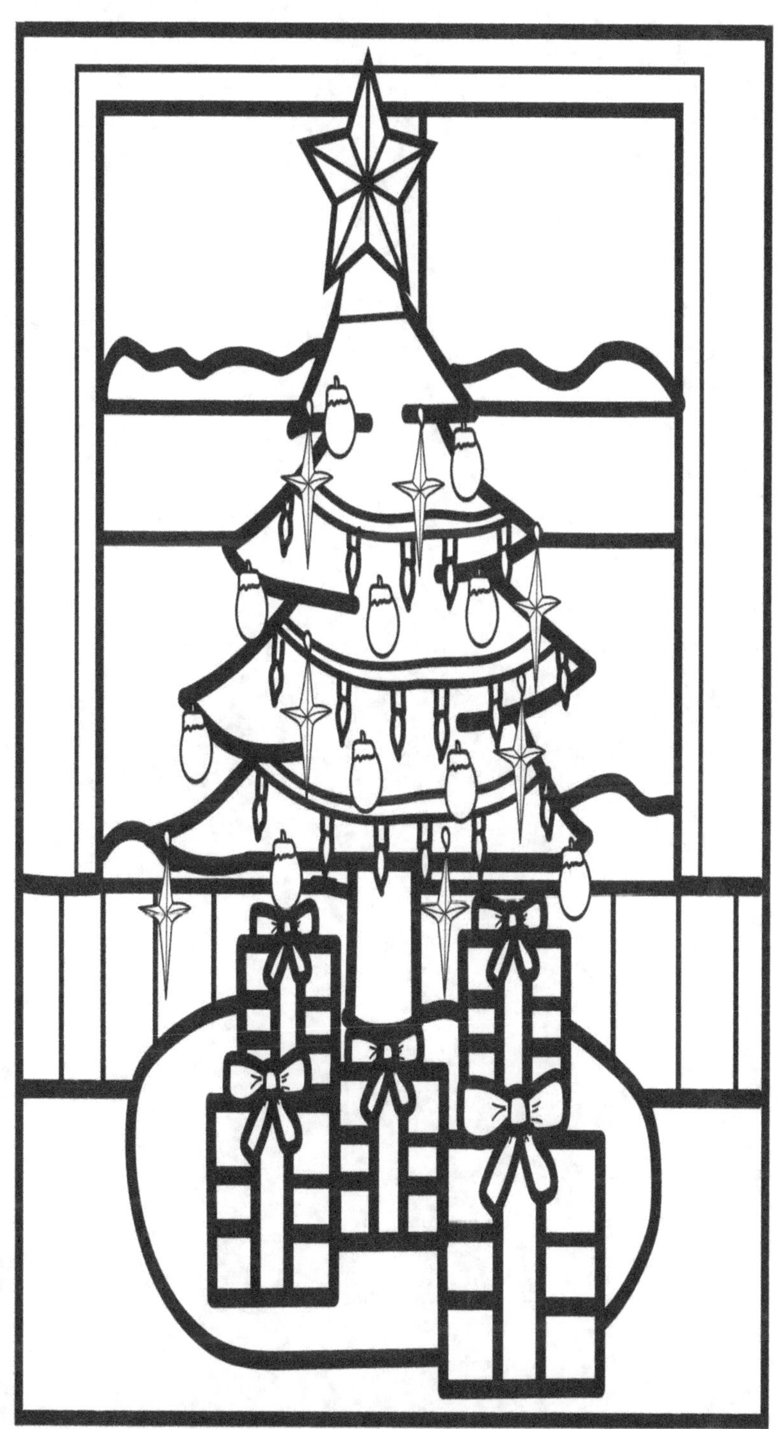

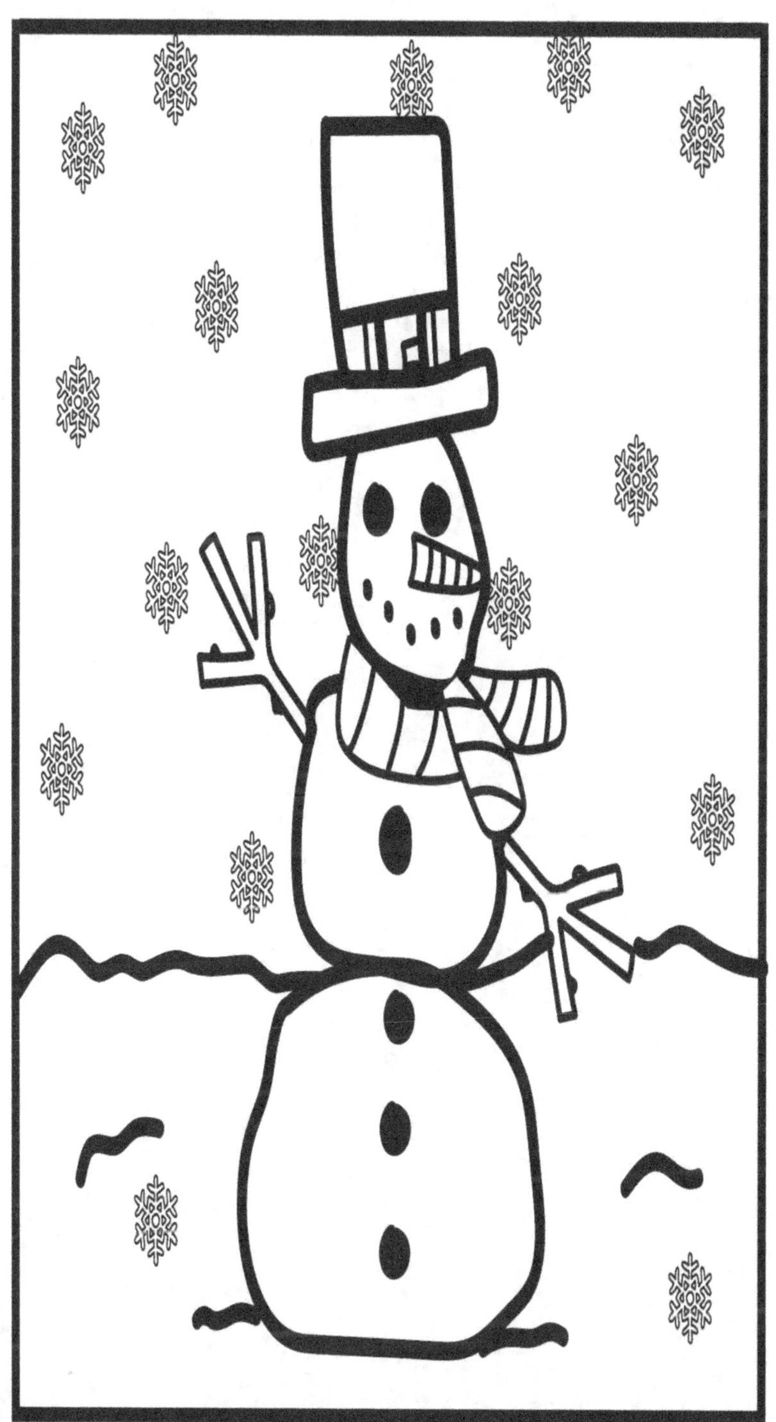

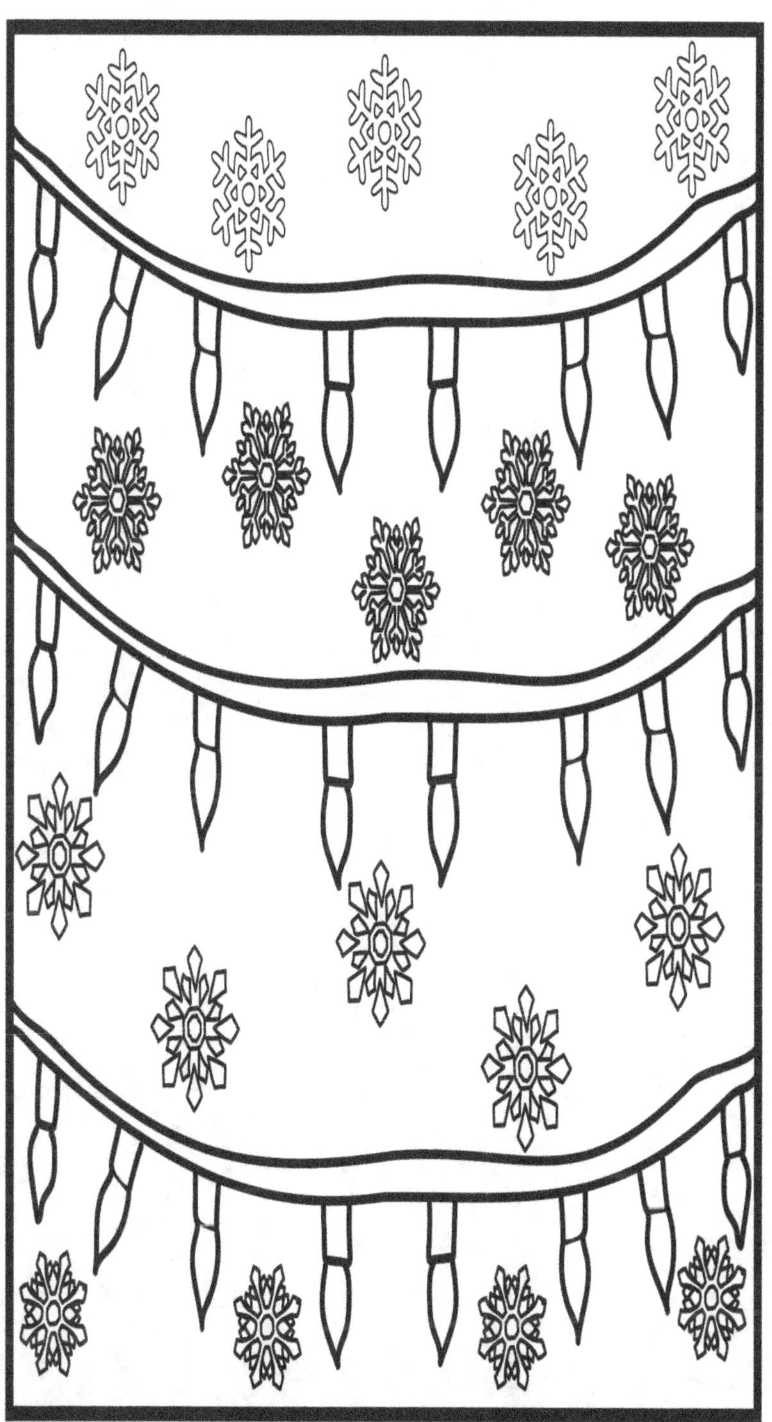

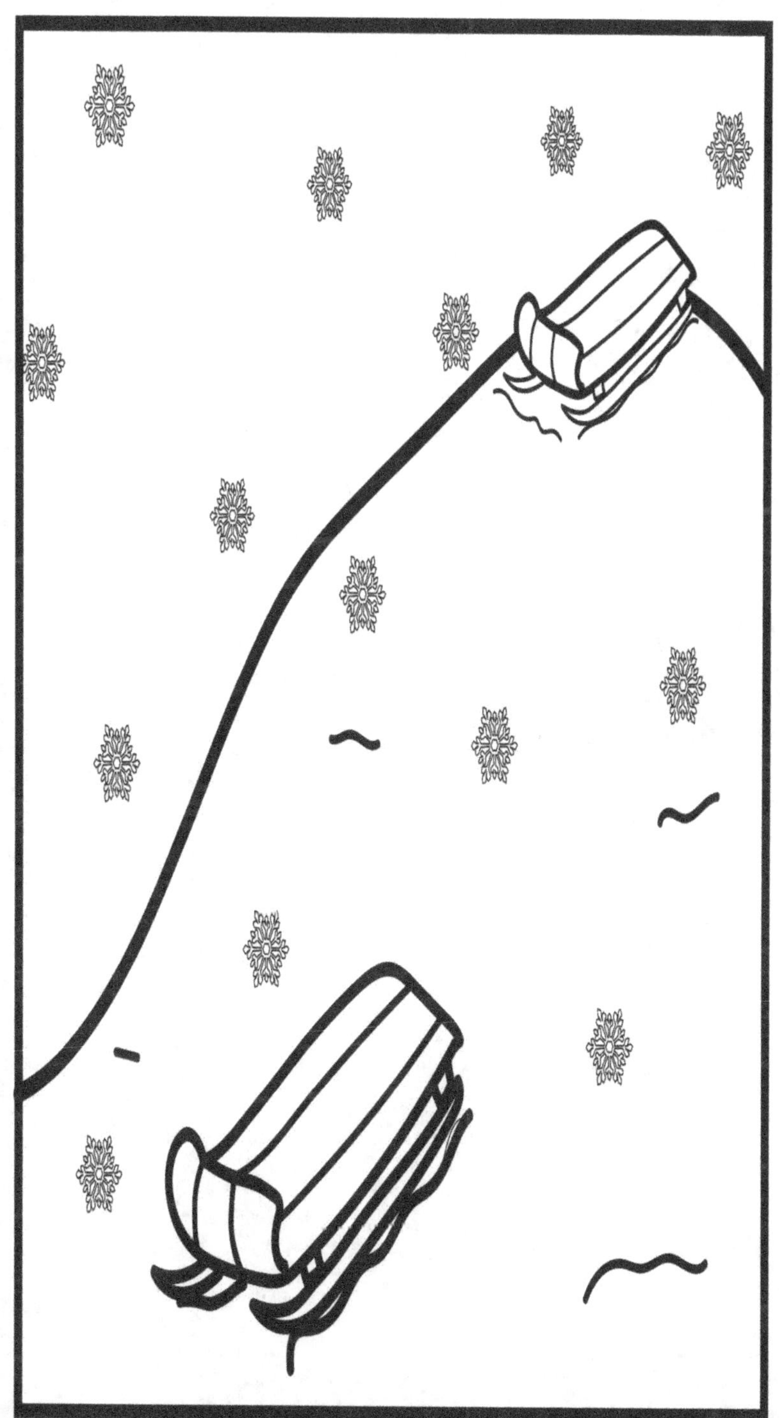

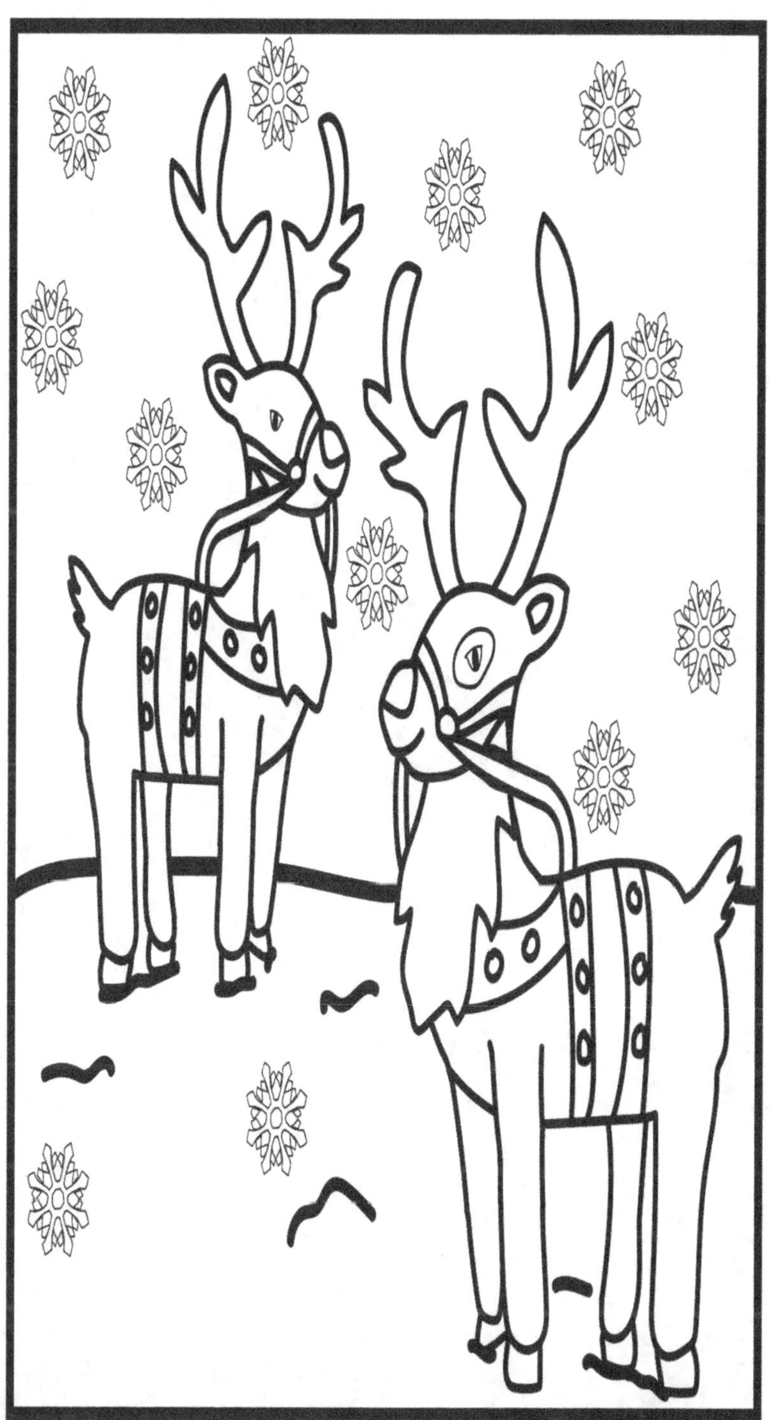

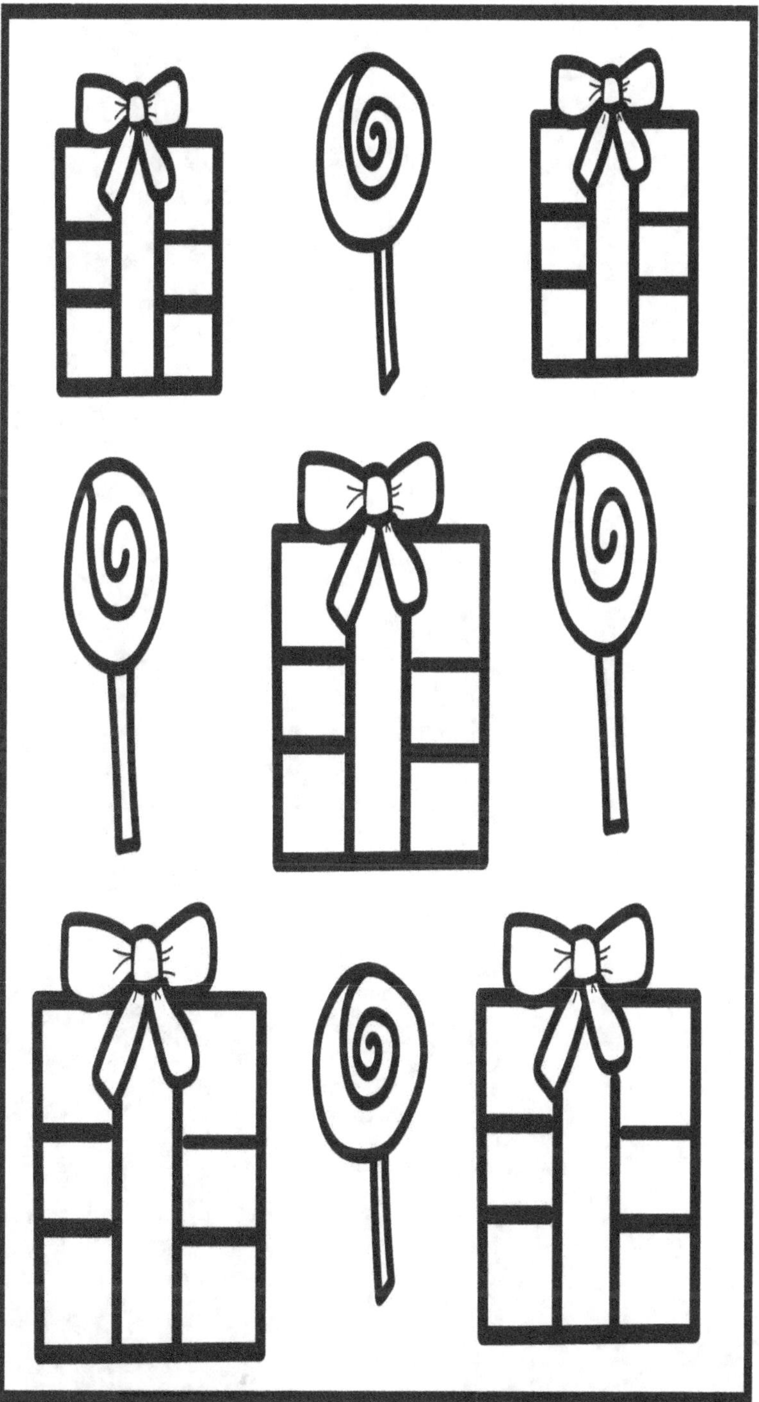

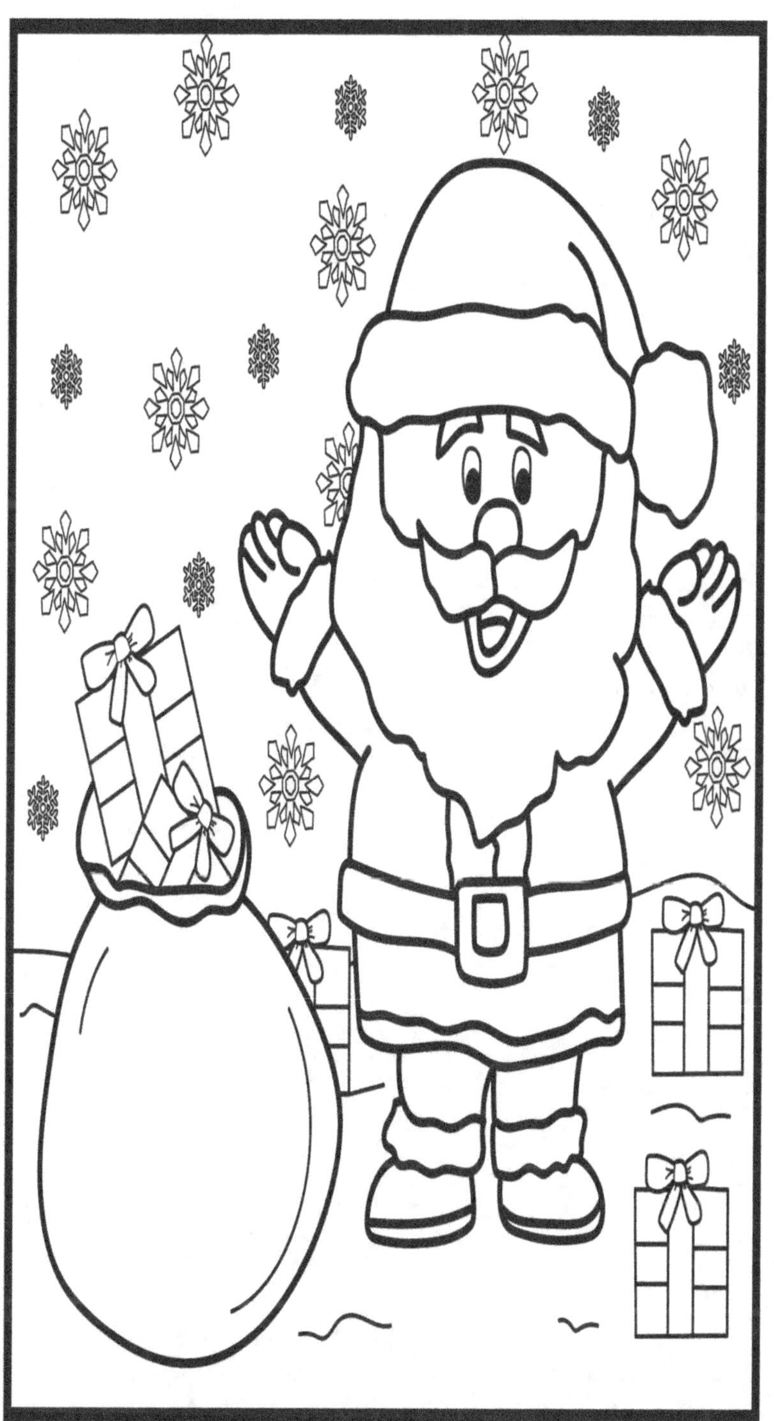

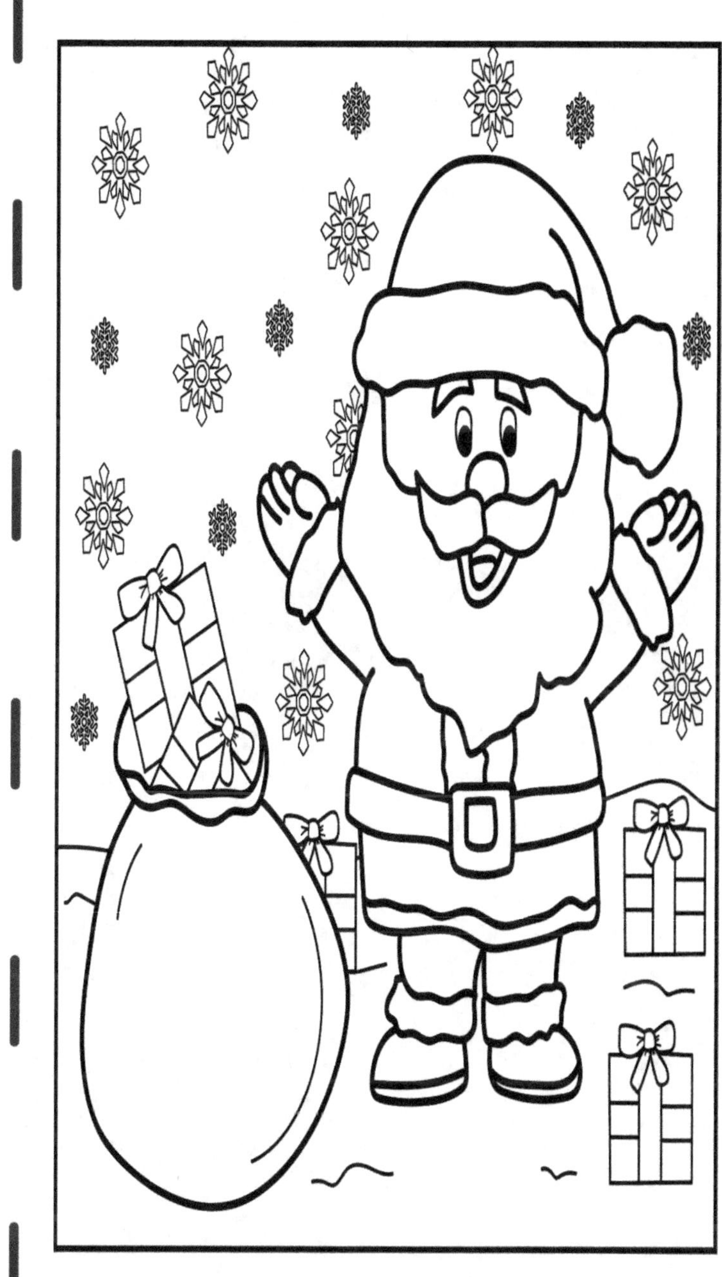

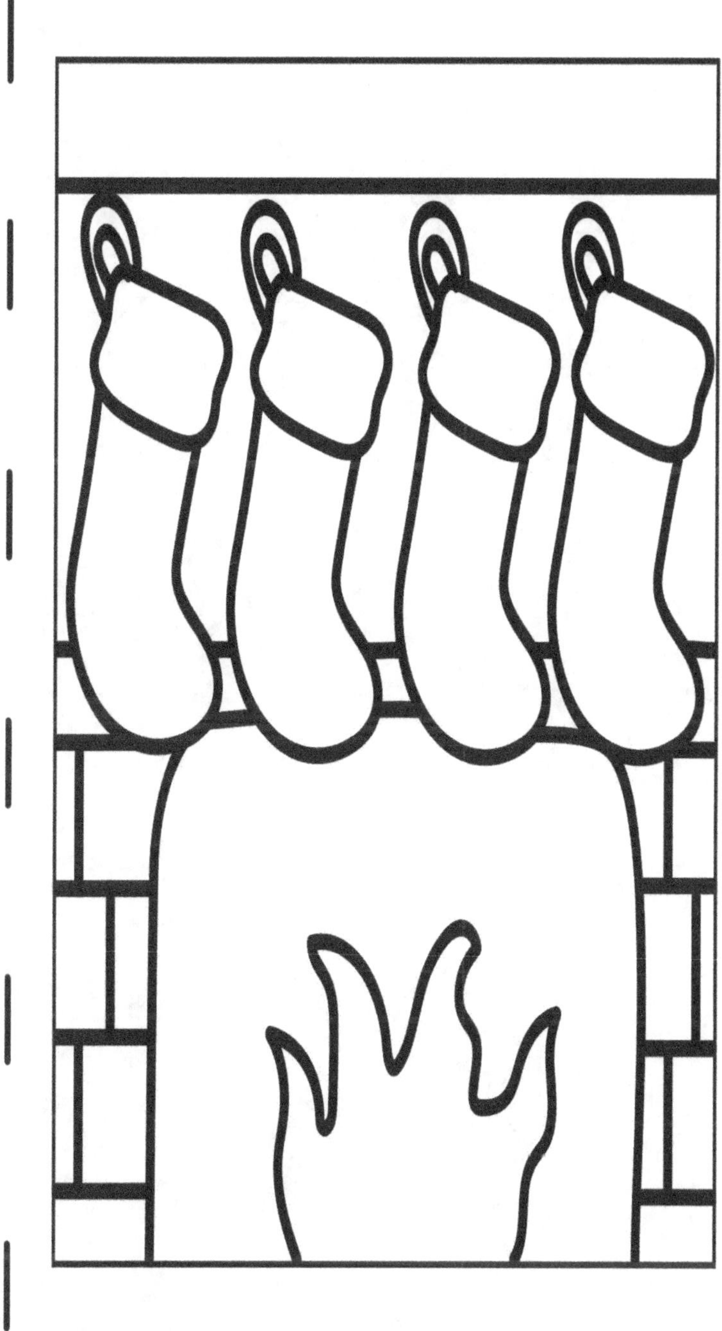

www.ingramcontent.com/pod-product-compliance
Lightning Source LLC
Chambersburg PA
CBHW071302130726
47998CB00003B/1297